The Old Key

A Traditional Collection

Yallery Brown	2
Sun, Moon, and Water	12
The Black Bull of Norroway	18
The War of the Birds and the Beasts	26
Aina-Kizz and the Bearded Bai	42
The Old Key	50

Yallery Brown

An Old British Story

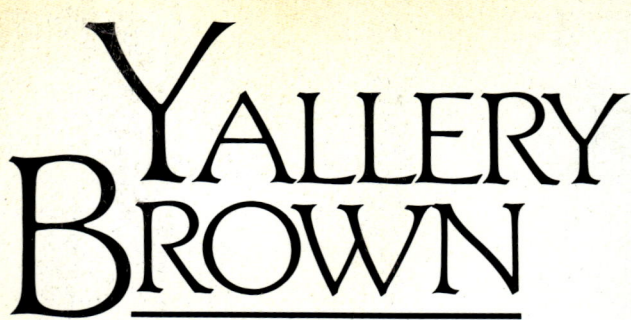

Once upon a time, and a very good time it was, though it wasn't in my time nor yet in your time, nor anyone else's time, there was a young lad of about eighteen or so, called Tom Tiver, who worked on the Hall's Farm. One Sunday he was walking across the west field. It was a beautiful, clear summer night, warm and still, and the air was full of little sounds as though the trees and grass were chattering to themselves.

All at once there came, a bit ahead of him, the most pitiful wailing ever he heard—sob, sobbing like a child beside itself with fear, and sounding just about heartbroken. It would give a low moan and then let out a long, whimpering wailing that made him feel sick in the stomach.

He began to look everywhere for the poor creature.

"It must be Sally Bratton's child," he thought to himself. "She was always a flighty thing, and never looked after it properly. As likely as not, she's out and about and has clean forgotten the baby." But though he looked and looked, he could see nothing.

Then the whimpering got louder and stronger in the quietness, and he thought he could just about make out some sort of words. He listened hard and the poor thing was saying words all mixed up with sobbing, "Ooh, the stone, the great big stone! Ooh, the stone on top!"

Naturally he wondered where the stone might be. He looked again, and there below the hedge was a great, flat stone almost buried in the dirt and hidden in among the ragged grass and weeds. This stone was the one people around there used to call "The Strangers' Table." The Strangers danced on it on moonlit nights, and it was never meddled with because you know it's bad luck to cross the Little People—the ones they called "The Strangers."

However, down he fell onto his knees beside the stone and listened again. Clearer than ever, but tired and weary with crying, came the little sobbing voice.

"Ooh, ooh! The stone, the stone on top!" Tom Tiver was afraid and didn't like to meddle with the thing, but he couldn't stand the whimpering baby. He tore like mad at the stone till he felt it lifting from the dirt. All at once it came out with a sigh, out of the dry earth and the tangled growing things.

And there in the hole lay a tiny thing on its back, blinking up at the moon and at him. It was no bigger than a year-old baby, but it had long, tangled hair and a beard twisted round and round its body so that you couldn't see its clothes. The hair was all yellow and shiny and silky like a child's, but the face of it was old as if it were hundreds of years since it was young and smooth. It was just a heap of wrinkles and two bright, black eyes in the midst, set in a lot of shining yellow hair. The skin was as brown as freshly plowed earth, brown as brown could be, and its feet and hands were brown like its face. The crying had stopped, but the tears were still on its cheeks; and the tiny thing looked all lost in the moonshine and in the night air. But although it was so tiny and old, Tom felt uneasy with it—unsure of what it would do.

The creature's eyes got used to the moonlight, and presently it looked up at Tom's face as bold as could be.

"Tom," said he, "you're a good lad!" And his voice was high and piping like a little bird twittering. Tom began to think what he should say; but he was rigid with fright, and he couldn't get a word out.

"Hoots," said the thing again. "You needn't be afraid of me; you've done me a better turn than you know, and I'll do a lot for you in return."

Tom couldn't speak yet, but he thought to himself, "This thing sure looks like one of those bogles I've heard about."

"No!" said the creature as quick as a wink, "I'm no bogle, but you'd best not ask me what I am; anyway I'll be a good friend of yours."

Tom's knee-bones knocked together, for it was certain that no ordinary body could have known what he was thinking to himself. But it looked so kind and spoke so warmly that Tom said bravely, even if his voice sounded rather trembly, "Might I ask Your Honor's name?"

"Hmm," it said, pulling its beard. "Well, as to that," and it thought for a bit. "Yallery Brown you may call me, Yallery Brown, yes indeed. It's what I am, you see, yaller and brown, and it'll do for a name well enough: Yallery Brown, Tom, Yallery Brown's yer friend, me lad."

"Thank you, master," said Tom all meekly.

"And now," he said, "I'm in a hurry tonight, but tell me quick, what'll I do for you? Do you want a wife? I'll get you the finest lass in town. Or do you want to be rich? I'll get you as much gold as you can carry. Or do you want help with your work? Just say the word!"

Tom scratched his head. "Well, as for a wife, I don't really have a yen for that. They're only a nuisance, and there are already plenty of folk at home to care for my needs. And as for gold—well I can take it or leave it. But as for work, now you're talking. I can't abide work, so if you'll give me a helping hand I'll thank…"

"Stop," said he as quick as lightning. "I'll help you, and welcome, but if ever you say that to me—if ever you thank me, do you see, you'll never see me more. Remember that now—I want no thanks; I'll have no thanks!"

And he stamped his little foot on the earth and looked as wicked as a raging bull.

"Remember that now, you great big lump of a thing," he went on, calming down a bit. "If ever you need help or get into trouble, call on me and just say, 'Yallery Brown, come from the ground, I want you,' and I'll be with you at once. And now," said he, picking up a dandelion puff, "goodnight to you." And he blew the puff and all the bits flew into Tom's eyes and ears.

As soon as Tom could see again, the tiny creature was gone, and except for the fact that the stone stood up on its end, and there was the hole at his feet, he'd have thought that he'd been dreaming.

Well, Tom went home to bed, and by morning he'd almost forgotten all about it. But when he went to work on the Monday morning, there was none to do! Everything had been done already—the horses seen to, the stables all cleaned out, everything in its proper place, nothing for him to do but stand around with his hands in his pockets.

And so it went on, day after day, all the work done by Yallery Brown, and done better, too, than he could have done it himself. And if Tom's master gave him more work, he just sat down while the work did itself. The rake or the brooms or what-not simply got on with it, with never a hand needing to touch them and the work was done in no time. He never saw Yallery Brown by daylight; only in the darkness he saw him hopping about like a will-o'-the-wisp without his lantern.

At first, it was mighty fine for Tom; he'd nothing to do and got good pay for it, but after a while things began to go a bit haywire. If the work was done for Tom, it was undone for the other lads; if his buckets were filled, theirs were upset; if his tools were sharpened, theirs were blunted and wrecked; if his horses were as clean as daisies, theirs were splashed with muck, and so on. Day in and day out, it was the same.

And what's more, the lads saw Yallery Brown flitting about at night, but in the daytime they saw the work being done without anyone's hands on the tools and Tom's work being done for him, and theirs undone for them. Naturally they began to avoid Tom; they wouldn't speak or come near him, and they told tales about him to their master. So things went from bad to worse.

For Tom could do nothing himself—the brooms wouldn't stay in his hand, the plow ran away from him, the rake wouldn't let him hold it. He decided that he wanted to do his own work after all, so that Yallery Brown would leave him

and his neighbors alone. But he couldn't—he could only sit and look on, and have the cold shoulder turned on him while that spooky thing was meddling with the others and working for him.

At last, things got so bad that the master gave Tom the sack, and if he hadn't, the rest of the lads would have sacked him, for they swore they wouldn't stay on the same patch with him. Well, naturally, Tom felt bad; it was a good place and the pay was good too; and he was mad with Yallery Brown, as he'd caused him so much trouble. So Tom shook his fist in the air and called out as loud as he could, "Yallery Brown, come from the ground; you scamp, I want you!"

You'll not believe this, but the words were hardly out of Tom's mouth when he felt something tweaking his leg from behind. He jumped with the sting of it, and when he looked down there was the tiny thing with his shining hair, wrinkled face, and wicked glinting black eyes.

Tom was in a fine rage and he would have liked to have kicked him, but that was no good, as there wasn't enough of the thing to get his boot into; but he said, "Look here, master, I'll thank you to leave me alone after this, do you hear? I want none of your help, and I'll have nothing more to do with you—so there!"

The horrid thing broke into a screeching laugh and pointed its sharp finger at Tom. "Ho, ho, Tom!" said he. "You've thanked me, me lad, and I told you, I told you not to!"

"I don't want your help, I tell you," Tom yelled at him. "I only want never to see you again, and to have nothing more to do with you. You can go!"

The thing only laughed and screeched and mocked as long as Tom went on shouting, but as soon as his breath gave out…

"Tom, me lad," he said with a grin. "I'll tell you something, Tom. True as true, I'll never help you again, and no matter how hard you call, you'll never see me again after today. But

I never said I'd leave you alone, Tom, and I never will, me lad. I was nice and safe under that stone, Tom, and could do no harm, but you let me out and you can't put me back again! I would have been your friend and worked for you if you'd been mine, but as you are no more than a fool, I'll give you no more than a fool's luck; and when everything goes haywire you'll remember that it's Yallery Brown at work."

Dancing around Tom, he began to sing, like a child with his yellow hair, but looking older than ever with his wrinkled bit of a face:

"Work as you will,
You'll never do well;
Work as you might,
You'll never do right;
For harm and mischief and Yallery Brown
You've let out yourself from under the stone."

Tom could never quite remember what he said next, but he was so amazed and fearful that he could only stand there shaking all over, staring down at the horrid thing. But after a while its yellow shining hair rose up in the air and wrapped itself round about it till it looked for all the world like a giant dandelion puff; and it floated away on the wind over the wall and out of sight with a horrid sneering laugh.

As for Tom, well, he worked here and he worked there and he turned his hand to this and to that, but things never went too well for him—and Tom always said that it was Yallery Brown's doing. But, mind you, he'd never been one for work in any case.

Sun, Moon and Water

An Old Tale from Nigeria

Many thousands of years ago, before human beings roamed the world, Sun and Moon were married and they lived together in a hut in Africa. They were quite content. They had one neighbor, Water, who lived far away from them in her own hut, and Sun would go to visit her from time to time, to make sure she was never too lonely. Then he returned to his wife, Moon, and through day and night he recounted the news that had passed between them.

One day when Sun was with Water, he said:

"Why is it that I am always coming to see you and you never repay us with your presence? Why not be a guest in our hut?"

"Ah," replied Water, a little wistfully, "I should love to meet your wife, Moon. I have heard so much about her. But I'm afraid your home may

not accommodate me and all the life I contain. You see, I bring with me so many fish of all sizes: whales and sharks of the ocean, salmon and trout, starfish, creatures that live in shells like the limpets, even the tiniest minnows."

"Do not let it worry you," said Sun boldly. "I will rebuild our hut. I will make it large enough to welcome you whenever you care to call."

He returned to Moon and told her what he planned to do, and Moon, watching his enthusiasm, hoped he was not getting carried away.

Immediately Sun began to build. He created a house so huge it stretched as far as the eye could see. Meanwhile, Moon prepared for the arrival of Water; and Water watched their home from afar, longing for the time when she could enter it.

At last the appointed hour arrived, and Sun and Moon stood at their sturdy new doorway watching. They saw Water moving. She was like a broad, gleaming mirror that grew and spread in all directions. Across the wide plains she came, swirling round the trees and lapping at the smooth rocks at the foothills of the mountains. On and on she flowed until she arrived at the feet of Sun and Moon.

"Here I am at your doorstep, dear neighbors, and how pleased I am to meet you," she said as she saw Moon smiling gently. "What a splendid home you have built, Sun. I am very honored."

"Won't you come in?" said Sun excitedly.

"I think I certainly shall," replied Water, "but we have not all arrived yet. Can you really fit us in?"

"Surely, surely," Sun replied, opening the door wider, and Water rose above the steps.

Water flowed freely through the house and began to mount the walls, which creaked and groaned with the pressure of her weight. Moon, sitting in a window frame, glared palely at her husband.

"I feel you're going to overflow us," she said, watching Water's slow ascent.

"Nonsense," Sun retorted. "These rooms are large enough for us all."

Moon turned to look outside. She saw how Water advanced slowly, steadily, spreading across the land. She didn't want to voice her dismay, but she noticed that the distant forests had now vanished from view and only the peaks of the mountains showed stark and clear above the dull, flat surface of her newly made friend, Water. Was she such a friend? It was Sun who had insisted on her visit. What if they drowned? She called to Sun to come and see, and he waded across the floor toward her, his toes only just reaching those planks he had thought so securely fastened. Now they seemed slippery. He felt the many fish brush against him as they darted madly from room to room.

"You are sure you can contain us?" murmured Water, hoping she was not imposing too much.

"Think nothing of it," replied Sun nonchalantly, though he realized now that he was obliged to swim, as his feet no longer reached the floor.

At the window, Sun and Moon stared at the bare, wet world outside. Now and then they saw a dolphin leap above the level line of water or a whale blow a single jet into the air before he sank and disappeared. Flying fish leapt about, playing in their newfound liberty.

"I am sure Water will overflow us," said Moon as she stood on the window frame and attempted to climb above the continually rising flood.

"But our home is so large—and we cannot offend our neighbor," Sun pleaded.

"Am I proving too difficult a guest?" asked Water.

Neither Sun nor Moon heard her. They had scrambled onto the

roof in a determined effort to save themselves from Water's ascent.

Water broke across the sloping thatch in waves that sent a spray of foam against the shivering bodies of Sun and Moon. They held each other tight, but soon Moon struggled from her husband in anger.

"We are being overflowed. We must escape," she cried. She looked about them and saw that the only space was immediately above. They leapt into the sky. Hundreds of thousands of miles their first step took them. They raced across the air at great speed. Finally, when they knew they were far enough away from her, they looked back to see how Water went on flowing, swirling across the earth, leaving only patches of land that were high enough to resist her spread.

Sun and Moon stayed in the sky. There they gave birth to their children, the stars, and would have remained quite happy had not Moon occasionally yearned to be back in their first home.

"I told you our house would be overflowed," she often repeated to Sun. And he, not liking to be reminded of their loss, grew angry with her. So real arguments grew between them. At times Moon, at her great distance, attempted to banish Water from the huge patches of earth she now inhabited. Water would fall away from the coasts, revealing the sand beneath her. But the effort tired Moon, and just as frequently Water slipped back to where she lapped along the shore. She could see Sun and Moon from wherever she roamed. She never quite understood why they had abandoned her.

But Moon was not able to forget a thing. She scolded her husband continuously, until late one evening she could bear his excuses no longer. She woke all her children, the stars, and quietly moved them with her to another part of the sky.

From then on, Sun searched for her, burning brightly to give himself light to find her. In the evening he was so exhausted that he dropped down in the West to seek some repose. It was then that Moon came out of hiding and urged the stars to follow her, though they scattered and danced, so glad were they to be free.

So the search goes on. Sun tours the sky, shining hard to find his wife, and Moon stays hidden until night. They may never meet again. But Water profits from the company of both her friends. In the day, she feels the warmth of Sun's light sparkling brilliantly upon her moving back. At night, she is cooled by the touch of Moon's shine. And Moon, because she is still so resentful, sometimes manages to hide from Water too. Then all is dark and black, and the earth must wait for the waking hours of Sun when he sets himself aglow, preparing for the chase of a new day.

The Black Bull of Norroway

An Old Scottish Story

In Norroway once there lived a certain woman, and she had three daughters. The oldest of them said to her mother, "Mother, bake me an oatcake and roast me some mutton, for I'm going away to seek my fortune."

Her mother did so, and the daughter went away to an old witch washer-wife to tell her of her intention. The old wife told her to stay that day with her and look out of the back door to see what she could see.

She saw nothing the first day. The second day she saw nothing. But on the third day she looked again and saw a coach and six horses coming along the road. She ran in and told the old wife what she saw.

"Oh, well," said the old wife, "that's for you."

So she was taken into the coach, and they galloped off.

The second daughter next said to her mother, "Mother, bake me an oatcake and roast me some mutton, for I'm going away to seek my fortune."

Her mother did so, and away she went to the old witch washer wife, as her sister had done. It was as it was before, and the third day she looked out of the back door and she saw a coach and four horses coming along the road.

"Oh, well," said the old wife, "that's for you." So they took her in and off they set.

The third daughter said to her mother, "Mother, bake me an oatcake, and roast me some mutton, for I'm going away to seek my fortune."

Her mother did so, and away she went to the old witch washer wife. She told her to look out of her back door to see what she could see. She did so, and when she came back she said that she saw nothing. The second day she did the same, and she saw nothing. The third day she looked again, and when she came back she said to the old wife that she saw nothing but a great black bull coming roaring along the road.

"Oh, well," said the old wife, "that's for you."

When she heard this, the girl was beside herself with grief and terror, but she was lifted up and put on the bull's back and away they went.

Long they traveled, and on they traveled, till the girl grew faint with hunger.

"Eat out of my right ear," said the bull, "and drink out of my left, and put aside what is left over."

So she did as he said and was wonderfully refreshed. And long they rode, and hard they rode, till they came in sight of a big and bonny castle.

"There we must stay this night," said the bull, "for there lives ny old brother," and soon they were at the place.

She was lifted off his back and taken in, and the bull was sent off to the park for the night. In the morning, when they brought the bull home, they took the girl into a fine, shining room and gave her a beautiful apple, telling her not to taste it until her heart was close to breaking. Then she was lifted onto the bull's back.

And after she had ridden far, and farther than I can tell, they came in sight of a far bonnier castle.

The bull said to her, "There we must stay this night, for my second brother lives there."

And they were at that place shortly. They lifted her down and took her in, and sent the bull to the field for the night.

In the morning, they took her into a fine room and gave her the finest pear she had ever seen, telling her not to taste it until her heart was close to breaking. Again she was lifted onto the bull's back and away they went.

Long they traveled, and on they traveled, till they came in sight of the far biggest castle, the farthest away they had yet seen.

And the bull said to her, "There we must stay this night, for my third brother lives there."

And they were straightaway at that place. They lifted her down and took her in, and sent the bull to a meadow for the night.

In the morning, they took her into a room, the finest of all, and gave her a plum, telling her not to taste it until her heart was close to breaking. Then they brought the bull home and set the girl on his back, and away they went.

And long they traveled, and on they traveled, till they came to a dark and ugsome glen, where they stopped, and the girl slid down.

The bull said to her, "You must stay here, while I go and fight the Old Feller. You must sit yourself on that stone and move neither hand nor foot till I come back, or I'll never find you again. And if everything around about you turns blue, I have beaten the Old Feller; but if everything turns red, he'll have beaten me."

She sat herself down on the stone, and after a while everything around her turned blue. She was filled with joy, and she lifted one foot and crossed it over the other, so glad she was that the bull had won. The bull came to look for her, but could find her nowhere.

Long she waited, and long she wept, till she was weary. At last she got up and moved on, she did not know where to. On she wandered till she came to a great hill of glass, which she tried every way to climb; but she was not able to. Around the bottom of the hill she went, looking for a way over, till she came to a blacksmith's house; and he promised that if she would work for him for seven years, he would make her iron shoes, with which she could climb over the glassy hill.

At the end of seven years she got her iron shoes, climbed the glassy hill, and came to the old witch washer-wife's house. There she was old about a fine, young man who had sent some bloodstained shirts to be washed, and whoever washed the shirts would be his wife.

The witch had washed; then she had set her daughter to washing. They had both washed and washed, hoping to claim the young man for the daughter; but no matter how hard they scrubbed, they could not remove a single stain.

At last, they put the girl to work. As soon as she began, the stains came out pure and clean, but the old witch made the young man believe that it was her own daughter who had washed the shirts.

So the young man and the daughter were to be married, and the girl was distraught at the thought of it.

Then she thought of her apple, and because her heart was close to breaking, she bit into the fruit. The apple was filled with gold and jewels, the richest she had ever seen, and she showed them to the daughter.

"I will give you all these," she said, "if you will put off your marriage for just one day and one night and allow me to go alone into his room."

The daughter took the gold and jewels, but the witch made a sleeping drink, and gave it to the young man. He drank it and slept until morning without waking once. And all the while the girl sobbed and sang:

> *"Seven long years I worked for thee,*
> *The glassy hill I climbed for thee,*
> *The bloody shirt I washed for thee—*
> *So wilt thou not waken and turn to me?"*

But he did not.

The next day the girl did not know what to do, for sorrow; she thought that her heart was close to breaking, so she broke the pear and found it filled with gold and jewels far richer than before. She took the gold and jewels to the witch's daughter, and the marriage

was put off for one day and one night, and she was let into the young man's room alone; but the old wife gave him another sleeping drink, and he again slept until morning without waking. And all the while the girl sobbed and sang as before:

*"Seven long years I worked for thee,
The glassy hill I climbed for thee,
The bloody shirt I washed for thee—
So wilt thou not waken and turn to me?"*

Still he slept, and she nearly lost hope altogether. But that morning the young man went out and he met a woodsman who asked him what the noise and sobbing was that he had heard all night coming from the young man's room. The young man said that he had heard no noise. But the woodsman said that it was so and told him that he had better stay awake and hear what it was.

The third time the girl thought that her heart was close to breaking, so she broke the plum; and inside she found gold and jewels by far the richest of all. She gave them to the daughter to put off the marriage for another day and another night, so that she could go alone to the young man's room.

The witch gave him another sleeping drink, but he said that he couldn't drink it without sweetening. And when she went away for some honey, he poured out the drink and so made the old witch think he had drunk it after all. Then the girl came in, and he pretended to be asleep. She sang and sobbed as before:

> *"Seven long years I worked for thee,*
> *The glassy hill I climbed for thee,*
> *The bloody shirt I washed for thee—*
> *O my bonny bull of Norroway,*
> *Wilt thou not waken and turn to me?"*

He heard and turned to her. She told him all that had happened to her, and he told her all that had happened to him. He had the old witch and her daughter banished, and he and the girl were married, and, for all I know, they are living happily till this day.

The War of the Birds and the Beasts

A Tale from Russia

There was a boy called Ivan who lived in a hut in the forest. And outside the hut, close by, a mouse and a sparrow lived in a nest together.

This was in the days before it had been settled who was to live on earth and who in trees. Birds and beasts and humans all lived on the ground together. Only the fish kept to themselves, because they were in the water.

The mouse and the sparrow lived in a nest in the ground, very warm and happy, and ate berries and grain side by side. The sparrow brought berries from the trees, and the mouse brought the berries that grow near the ground, and grains of corn, and all the other things that a mouse can get without wings.

All went well until one day when they were having their dinner. It was like this. They had a pile

of berries and grain between them, and every time the mouse took a berry, so did the sparrow. And when the sparrow took a grain, the mouse took one also. In this way, no one got more than his share. But it so happened that when they had done sharing there was one little shining grain of corn left over.

"That should be mine," said the mouse.

"It should be mine," said the sparrow.

"But," said the mouse, "I fetched it."

"You did, did you," said the sparrow, "but who fetched the berries?"

"Let's share it," said the mouse.

"I'll bite it in half," said the sparrow, "and so we shall not quarrel."

So the sparrow took the grain of corn in his beak. It was very hard and very slippery. He tossed up his head, to get it to one side of his beak, and before he could stop it, it had slipped down his throat.

And there was the mouse watching him and waiting for his share.

"Where is it?" said the mouse.

"I've swallowed it," said the sparrow.

"You have, have you?" said the mouse ruffling his fur.

"It was a mistake," said the sparrow.

"Easy to say that, with a good grain of corn already in your greedy gullet," said the mouse.

And, with that, the mouse ran at the sparrow and bit him in the leg. And the sparrow hopped on one foot and beat the mouse with his wings. From the noise they made, they might have been a hundred times as big.

And Ivan heard the noise and came out of his hut, and there they were, fighting like anything, and calling each other names.

He was not the only one who heard them.

The rabbit heard them and ran to help the mouse. The blackbird heard them and flew to help the sparrow.

They fought too, and the noise was louder than ever and was heard by the pigeon and the

hare. They took a hand. Then came the dog and the rooster, the cat and the owl, the fox and the hawk, the rat and the robin, the bull and the swan. The mouse fought the sparrow. The rat fought the robin. The rabbit fought the blackbird. The hare fought the pigeon. The dog fought the hen. The fox fought the hawk. The cat fought the owl. The bull fought the swan. And other beasts fought other birds. They pranced and flapped and bit and pecked and screamed and barked and squealed and bellowed together.

And Ivan stood behind a tree, where he could see well and be safely out of the way.

The noise they made brought bigger beasts to the battle. And bigger birds came flying from far away to fight the bigger beasts. The nest of the mouse and the sparrow was trodden under foot by the wild boar as it fought with the solan goose. But neither the mouse nor the sparrow noticed that, for they were fighting, blinded in a little

whirlwind of flying feathers and fur.

Suddenly a dreadful stillness fell upon the forest.

The beasts stopped fighting, and bent their heads to the ground, and put their tails between their legs, and waited, trembling. For the earth was shaking with the coming of the Bear, the Tzar of all the beasts. And the birds stopped fighting and stood there, trembling, and ruffling out their feathers; such feathers as they had left, and waited. For the air was shaken with the coming of the Fire-Bird, the Tzar of all the birds.

There was such silence in the forest that Ivan heard a leaf hit the ground as it dropped from a tree.

Then the Bear swung heavily through the undergrowth, and stood there, looking at all the beasts and birds. And the beasts crawled with their bellies on the ground, and got behind the Bear, and waited, panting after the fight, and looking with red frightened eyes to see what would happen to the birds.

Then the Fire-Bird flew through the tall trees, like a great torch flung through the green dusk of the forest. And the birds fluttered away behind the Fire-Bird, and put their heads under their wings, and shivered the feathers on their trembling bodies. And the Fire-Bird, golden and scarlet, with burning breast and gleaming wings, was alone before the Bear.

Then began the fight.

The Bear raised himself on his hind legs, and growled terribly, and lifted his black lips so that his white teeth shone red in the firelight that fell upon them from the burning breast of the Fire-Bird. The Fire-Bird spread wide his gleaming wings and rose into the air and came down upon the head of the Bear. The Bear yelled in pain from the scorching of his eyes and beat off the Bird with slow heavy blows of his great paws. The claws of the Bear were claws of steel, and the ground was red and gold with the feathers of the Bird.

Long they fought.

The hair of the Bear was singed to his skin and as he fought, he groaned in his pain. The Fire-Bird fought silently, beating the Bear with his golden wings, and scorching him with the burning feathers of his breast. And the beasts whimpered as they watched and heard the groaning of their Tzar. And the birds trembled where they stood. And the earth of the forest shook with the trampling of the Bear, and the roots of the trees were loosened in the ground. A wild wind drove through the forest, now this way, now that, from the beating of the Fire-Bird's wings, and the tall trees waved before it like fine grass.

At last the Fire-Bird pressed his burning breast on the head of the Bear and blinded him. The Bear in his great pain rolled on the ground, taking the Fire-Bird with him. One of the golden wings was broken in that rolling. The Fire-Bird could fight no more. The Bear, blinded and scorched, could fight no more. He stood there, groaning, while the beasts whimpered about him. Then he lumbered heavily away into the forest. The bull shook his great head and went off among the trees, swinging his angry tail. The wolf and the fox and the hare and the rabbit and the rat and the wild boar went their ways. The wild goose and the swan rose in the air and flew back to the marshlands. The hawk and the owl flew off, the hawk high above the forest, the owl still keeping in the shadow of the great trees. One by one the beasts and the birds were gone, and at last none was left but the mouse and the sparrow, and the Fire-Bird with his broken golden wing.

The boy, Ivan, stepped from behind the tree and came to the Fire-Bird lying there on the ground. The mouse and the sparrow huddled together. Their nest had been trodden under foot by the wild boar, and they had nowhere to live.

"And all for a grain of corn," chirped the sparrow.

"And the Bear, the great Tzar of the Beasts, is blinded and burned," squeaked the mouse.

"And the Fire-Bird, before whose coming the forest itself is silent, has a broken wing," said the sparrow.

"And our home is gone," said the mouse.

"If only I had not lived with you," said the sparrow.

"You shall not live with me again," said the mouse.

And, with that, the mouse burrowed a hole for himself under Ivan's hut. And the sparrow made a nest for himself in a hole in the wall.

But Ivan cut the bough of a tree, and took ropes of bast, and bound the broken wing of the Fire-Bird to the bough, so that the wing should mend.

Said he: "If you lie quiet for a day or two, you'll be flying as well as ever, and in the meantime we can keep each other company."

The sparrow was taking a beakful of moss to his nest. "Do you hear that?" he said to the mouse, who was sitting at the mouth of his hole, cleaning his whiskers. "That boy is not afraid even of the Fire-Bird."

"Why should he be afraid of him?" squeaked the mouse. "The Bear broke his wing."

"Aye, and went off with blind eyes and no hair," said the sparrow.

They would have fought again. But, just as they were going to fight, the mouse looked at the sparrow, and said: "If we fight, the others will come and fight too, and this time, who knows? They may trample the hut itself to pieces."

"True," said the sparrow, and flew to his nest in the wall, while the mouse ran back to his hole.

The Fire-Bird lay in Ivan's hut. A week he lay there, and covered his breast with his good wing, lest the heat of his burning breast should turn the hut to cinders. His broken wing mended. And on the eighth day the Fire-Bird strutted gloriously out of the hut into the sunlight, and the mouse looked from his hole, and the sparrow from his nest, to see the sunlight on the Fire-Bird's gleaming feathers.

"Do you think you can fly now?" said Ivan, and the Fire-Bird did not answer but shook his mighty wings. He looked around at the broken trees and trampled earth where the Beasts had fought with the Birds. And the flames in his eyes twinkled, and he said to Ivan: "Up on my back, Ivan, and we will find something to put on this open ground."

Ivan sat on the back of the Fire-Bird between his golden wings, and the Fire-Bird flew up out of the clearing in the forest and over the tops of the tall trees. And down below in the forest, the beasts grumbled silently to themselves as they heard the flapping of his wings, and blinked when they looked up through the leaves and saw him pass far overhead like a blazing bit of the sun. The blind Bear growled under his breast and lifted his scorched head, and a ray of heat from the burning breast of the Bird fell on the Bear's head, and the Bear put his head between his paws, and whimpered wretchedly. But Ivan, sitting up there between the wings of the Fire-Bird, sang aloud as they flew through the blue air, beyond the forest, beyond the plains, beyond the blue hills, and the marshlands and the sea that lie behind the hills.

And the Fire-Bird said to Ivan: "Look down, and tell me what you see."

And Ivan looked, and said: "There is a palace by the seashore."

"It is the palace of my eldest sister," said the Fire-Bird. "We will rest there, and drink tea with my eldest sister."

The Fire-Bird dropped from the sky like a falling star, while Ivan caught his breath.

In the doorway of the palace stood a Princess, as straight as a fir and as slender as a birch tree. She moved like a woman, but she was made of fine gold, and her bare arms shone in the sunlight, like the feathers of the Bird, her brother.

"Welcome, brother," said the Princess of gold, and went before them into the palace, and called for a samovar and two glasses, one for herself and the other for the Fire-Bird.

"And a third glass for Ivan," said the Fire-Bird.

The Princess stiffened like a gold statue.

"I will not drink with him," said she, and stood there scornful, because she was a Princess, and her brother was the Fire-Bird, and Ivan was a poor peasant lad.

The gold feathers of the Fire-Bird rustled with anger, and he went back into the courtyard. "Away," said he, and Ivan climbed up and sat again between his wings.

Then the Fire-Bird rose like a flaming eagle, up, up, into the sky above the palace.

"Watch now," said he to Ivan when he was high in the sky, hovering like a blazing hawk.

With that he bent his head and thrust his beak deep into his burning breast and plucked a feather and let it go. Ivan watched it falling, scarlet and gold, like a feather of blood and flame. It fell, and almost before it touched the palace roof, the whole palace took fire and burned up in a single monstrous flame. The flame died as swiftly as it rose, and left nothing but a dark place of ashes on the gold shore of the sea.

They flew on. Evening fell. The sun went down and the moon rose. Once more the Fire-Bird asked Ivan what he saw.

And Ivan, leaning forward, looked down beneath the neck of the Bird and his great golden shoulder and saw another palace, carven and glittering pale in the moonlight, in the middle of a great plain.

"That is the palace of my second sister," said the Fire-Bird. "We will rest there and drink tea."

Again they flew down and alighted in the courtyard of the palace. The moonlight fell on its carven roofs, and in its doorway stood a Princess of silver, with her silver arms clasped behind her head, as she was looking at the moon.

"Welcome, brother," said she, and went before them to call for the samovar. "Two glasses," said she.

"Three," said the Fire-Bird.

"There is no third here who may drink with you and me," said the Princess in her slow proud voice.

And with that the Fire-Bird turned from her, saying not a word. And Ivan sat between the wings as he flew up again, high in the air between the earth and the moon. Once more the Fire-Bird plucked a feather from his breast, and it fell, blazing, through the night, and that palace, like the first, was burned up in a single sudden flame.

They flew on through the night. The moon went down, the stars paled and flickered out, and the dawn spread over the sky. Once more the Fire-Bird told Ivan to look down. Ivan leaned forward over the great golden shoulder of the Bird, and shielded his face from the heat of his burning breast, and saw mountains far below, and lakes, and in the heart of the mountains, a palace. The palace was of bronze with green roofs just touched with the first rays of the sun. And in the doorway of the palace was a little Princess of fine copper, lifting her metal arms to the dawn.

"That is the palace of my little youngest sister," said the Fire-Bird as he flew down out of the sunlight.

"Welcome, brother," said the little Princess, "and who is your guest?"

"This is Ivan, who healed my wing when it was broken in fighting with the Bear."

"He is welcome," said the little Princess, and threw her copper arms about Ivan's neck and kissed him on both cheeks. And her kiss was the kiss of a young girl, and her arms were soft about his neck.

The sun rose higher. The samovar was brought out into the courtyard, and they drank tea there in the sunshine, Ivan, the Fire-Bird, and the little Princess. All day long they drank tea and feasted together.

At evening the Fire-Bird stretched his golden wings. "Up on my back, Ivan," said he. "And you, little sister, pack him a palace in a wooden box, for we have some open ground to cover, where the trees were trodden under in the fight."

"I will give you my own," said the little Princess, and, with that, she clapped her hands. The palace grew littler and littler. When it was small enough, she picked it up and put it in a wooden box and gave it to Ivan.

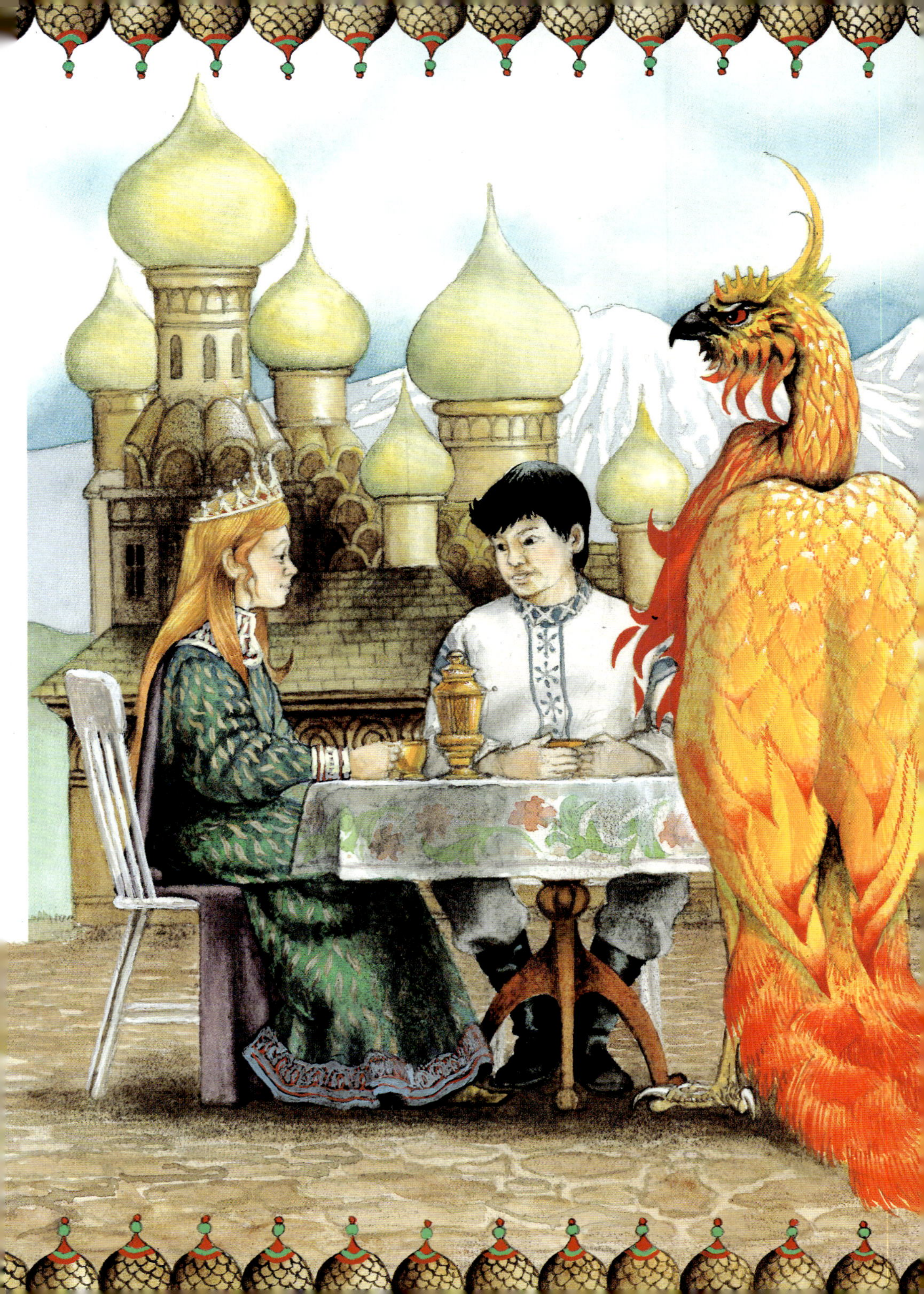

"But where will you live?" said Ivan.

"I shall have to come with you," said the Princess.

So they climbed up on the back of the Fire-Bird, and sat there with their arms about each other's waists, holding the box with the palace on their knees.

As the sun set, the Fire-Bird flapped his great gold wings and flew up into the dusky sky, and so through the night, like a flying fire. They flew through the moonlight and the dark and, next day in the sunlight, flew down to the forest and the trampled open ground where the Beasts had fought with the Birds.

There was silence in the forest as the Fire-Bird flew above the trees. There was silence when he flew down to Ivan's hut. The sparrow sat silent in his nest in the wall, and the mouse trembled in his hole under the hut.

Ivan and the Princess opened the box and took out the palace. One of its towers had been chipped on the journey, but they soon mended that. Then the Princess clapped her hands, and the little palace grew bigger and bigger and bigger until it was as big as it had been when Ivan and the Fire-Bird came flying down to it in the dawn. Then it stopped growing. Ivan and the Princess were just going to walk in, when they looked around for the Fire-Bird.

He was gone. While the palace was growing, he had flapped his great golden wings and flown away over the tops of the tall trees.

Just then, as the Fire-Bird was gone, all the birds in the forest began to sing. The beasts moved again in the undergrowth. The sparrow flew chirping from the wall of the hut and began to build a nest for himself under the roof of the palace. The mouse ran out squeaking, ran into the palace in front of Ivan and the little Princess, and found a snug hole for himself near the larder.

Ivan and the Princess went into the palace and drank tea and ate cakes and told stories to each other. They settled down and lived there very happily. The Fire-Bird never came again, nor will he until there is another war between the Birds and the Beasts. And that is not likely, because since that time the Birds and Beasts no longer live together. The Birds live in trees and under the roofs of palaces and huts and windmills, while all the four-footed Beasts live on the ground. The sparrow lives in the roof of Ivan's palace, and the mouse close by the larder. They no longer share their food. And so there are no more battles between the Birds and the Beasts.

Aina-Kizz and the Bearded Bai

A Story from India

There once was a young girl who lived with her father, a woodcutter, in an old tumbledown shack. They owned nothing between them but a lame old horse, a mule, and a gap-toothed saw. But as the old saying goes:

*A rich family's fortune is in its herds,
a poor family's fortune is in its children.*

And sure enough, whenever the old woodcutter looked at his daughter, who was only nine, he forgot all his worries and woes. The girl's name was Aina-Kizz, and she was so clever that people came from great distances to ask her advice.

One day, after the woodcutter had loaded his horse with logs for the market, he said to the girl, "I expect to be home by dusk, and if I sell any logs I'll bring you back a small present."

"Good luck then, Father," she replied, "but do take care:

One man's gain is another man's loss."

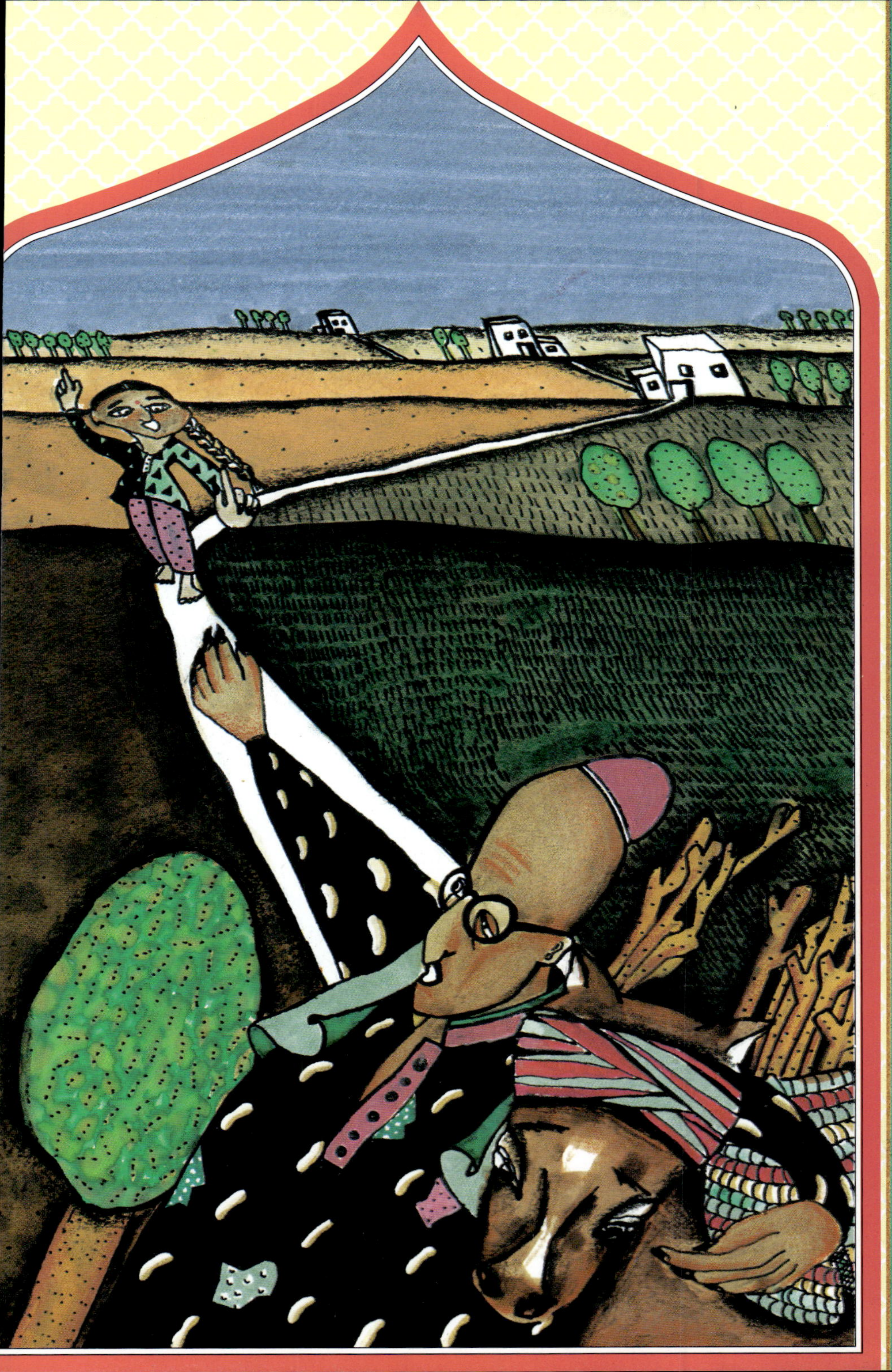

The woodcutter went on his way and arrived at the village in time for the bazaar; he stood beside his horse and waited for someone to buy his wood. But no one came. As it was getting late, a rich bai came strutting through the bazaar, flaunting his silk robe and stroking his sleek black beard. When he caught sight of the poor man and his load of logs he called, "Hey, woodcutter, old man, what will you take for your logs?"

"A single tanga, sir."

"Will you sell the wood exactly as it is?" he asked with a sly smirk.

The woodman nodded uncertainly, for he was not sure what he meant.

"Here's your tanga," said the bai, tossing down a coin. "Bring your horse and follow me."

When they came to the bai's large house, the woodman began to unload the logs. But the bai shouted, "Stop! I bought the wood 'exactly as it is,' which means that the horse is mine since it is carrying the wood. If you've any complaints, we'll go to the judge."

There is an old saying:
> *Just as a bad rider can turn a fine horse into a useless nag, so a bad judge can turn right into wrong.*

And so it was.

After listening to the two complaints the judge stroked his beard, looked sideways at the bai's silk robe, and gave his verdict: "The woodman has got what he deserves. It served him right for agreeing to the bai's terms!"

The rich man laughed in the woodman's face; and the woodman, poor man, trudged wearily home to tell the news to Aina-Kizz.

"Never mind, Father, I'll go to market tomorrow," she said. "You never know, I may be luckier than you."

Next day, she rose at dawn and loaded up the mule with logs. By pulling and coaxing the animal she managed to make her way to the bazaar. She stood beside the mule, and sure enough, the very same bai approached her.

"Hey, girl, what will you take for your load of wood?" he cried.

"Two tangas."

"And you will sell it exactly as it is."

"Certainly, provided you pay the money exactly as it is."

"Sure, sure," said the bai, holding out his hand to show her two gold coins. "Follow me."

The same thing happened to her as it had to her father. But she was not worried. The scheming bai went to give her the two coins, but she said, "Sir, you bought my wood just as it is, and you have taken my mule together with the wood.

But you promised to pay the money exactly as it is. So now I want your arm as well."

The bai was shaken. His beard trembled with rage; he cursed her soundly, but she stood her ground. At last they went together before the judge. The judge listened to the complaint, but this time he wasn't able to help the bai; he ruled that he must pay two tangas for the wood and another fifty in place of his arm.

The rich man was furious; he wished that he had left wood, horse and mule alone! As he handed over the money, he said to the girl, "You outwitted me this time, but

A sparrow is no match for a hawk.

I bet you can't tell a bigger lie than I can! I'll put five

hundred tangas on it. You put fifty and whoever the judge thinks tells the bigger lie wins the bet."

"Done!" said Aina-Kizz.

So, winking at the judge, the bai began his tale.

"One day, before I was born, I found three ears of corn in my pocket and tossed them out the window. Next morning, there was such a thick field of corn in my yard that it took ten days for a group of horsemen to find their way through it. By that time, forty of my best goats were lost in the corn. No matter how hard I searched, I couldn't find them. They'd vanished without a trace.

"Late in the summer, when the corn was ripe, my workmen gathered in the harvest and ground the flour. They made bread and I ate a loaf, fresh and hot. And what do you think? Goats began to leap out of my mouth—one by one, out came all the forty goats, bleating as they leapt. They'd all got as fat as a four-year-old bull!"

When the bai stopped talking, even the judge was speechless. But Aina-Kizz didn't turn a hair.

"Sir," she said, "wise men such as yourself can tell really grand lies. Now, please listen to my very humble tale."

Then she told her story.

"One day I planted a cotton seed in my garden. And the next day a cotton bush had grown so high that it touched the clouds; its shadow fell as far as three days' journey across the sands. When the cotton was ripe, I picked it and cleaned it and sold it in the market. With the money I got for it I bought forty camels. I loaded them all up with priceless silks and asked my brother to take them and sell them at the market in Samarkand.

"Off he went, dressed in his best silk robe; and then I heard nothing from him for three whole years. But, just recently, I heard that he had been robbed and killed by a bai. I gave up hope of finding his murderer, but now by chance I have discovered him. Is it you, bai, for you are wearing my brother's best silk robe!"

GOLD RUPEE
GOLD RUPEE
GOLD RUPEE
GOLD RUPEE
GOLD RUPEE
GOLD RUPEE
GOLD RUPEE
GOLD RUPEE

At these words, the smiles on the men's faces quickly changed to frowns. What could the judge say? If the story was a whopping lie, the bai would lose his five hundred coins—that was the bet. But if it was the truth…then he would have to charge him as a murderer; not to mention having to make him pay for the stolen forty camels loaded with silk.

The bai let out a load roar, "Liar! Liar! That's the biggest lie I've ever heard! Here, take your five hundred tangas, take my silk robe, only get out and leave me in peace."

Aina-Kizz smilingly counted her coins, then she wrapped them in the silken robe and walked back home.

The woodman had been afraid for his daughter and was waiting anxiously at the door to greet her. He hugged her happily and didn't even notice the missing mule.

"Father," she said, "I had to sell the mule with the logs, exactly as it was."

"Oh, my poor daughter," he muttered. "So that wretched bai has swindled you as well?"

"But I did receive a fair price for the wood," she said quietly. Then she handed him the robe.

"This is a fine robe," he said sadly. "But what use is it to me? We haven't even a horse or a mule, and likely as not we'll soon starve to death."

Then Aina-Kizz unrolled the robe in front of her father, and the gold coins tumbled out onto the floor. He didn't know whether to laugh or cry—so he did both! Then she told him all that had happened, and when she had finished she said:

"Where the rich keep their fortunes, the poor keep their wits.
A girl's wise head is better than a man's full purse."

The Old Key

A Tale from Turkey

In a country far from you and far from me there was once a great famine, and in that year everyone suffered terribly from hunger. The country people went down to the cities seeking food and work; among them was a good and handsome youth whose name was Abbas. Abbas had grown up in the care of a farmer, for when he was a baby his parents had died. Now the farmer was hungry and idle like all the rest, and since he could no longer feed Abbas he was forced to send him away.

So Abbas went away over the mountains, up hill and down dale, until at last he came to a city. He looked for somewhere to sleep the night, but although he searched everywhere there was not a spare place to be found. He remembered passing an old, ruined castle on his way to the city, so he retraced his steps and went back to the castle, where he settled down for the night among the ruins.

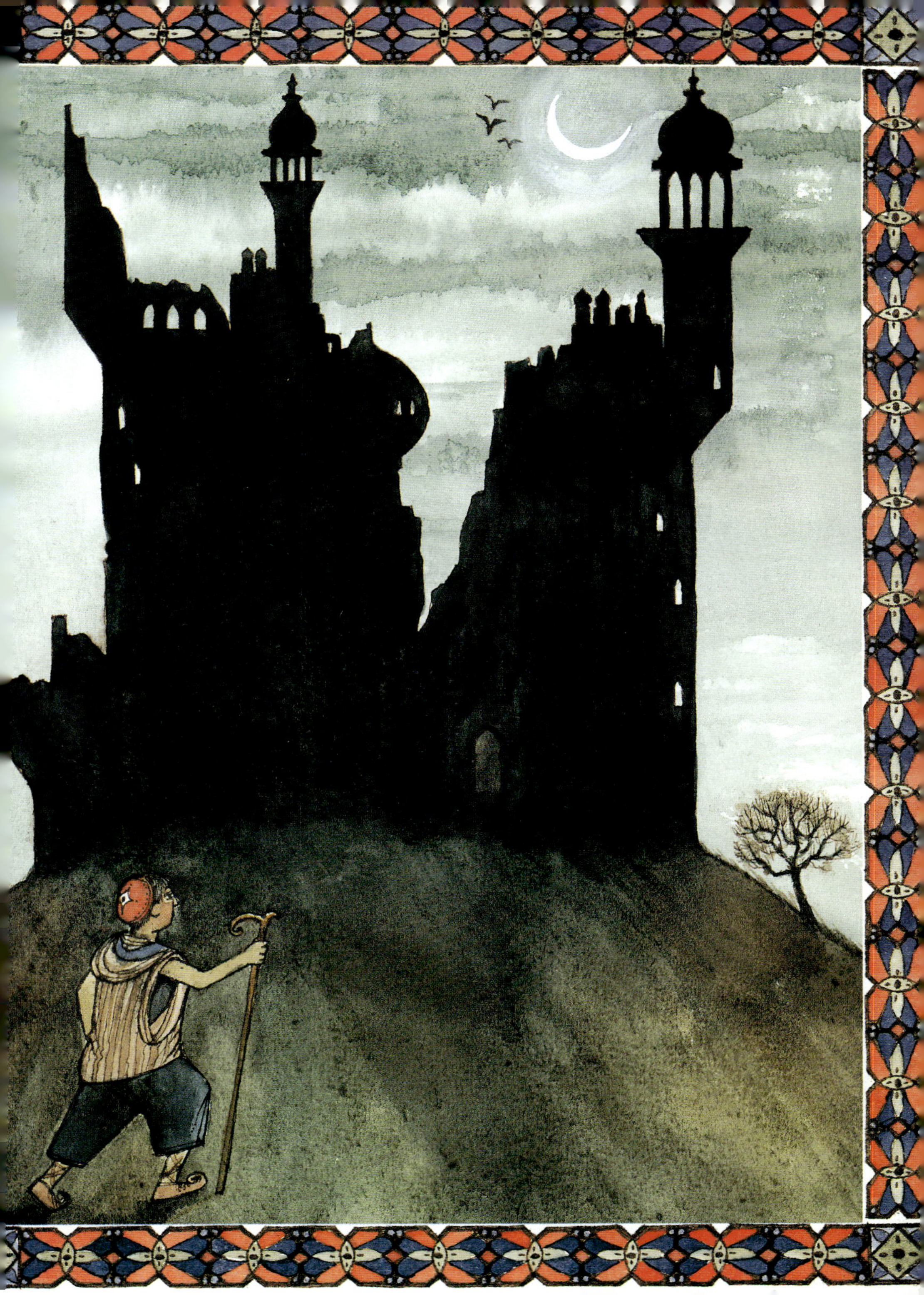

No sooner had Abbas closed his eyes in sleep than he felt something resting on his shoulder. He opened his eyes and saw a hand. It was holding a lighted candle. Then the hand began to move. Abbas got up and followed the light, which led him underneath the ruins into a great palace. There he saw a table laden with a thousand sorts of food, which he began to eat hungrily.

Then the hand moved on. Abbas was curious to find out where it would lead him, so he followed it. He came to a beautifully decorated room in which there was a finely carved, four-poster bed. He undressed, put on a silk dressing gown that was lying on the bed, lay down between the cool sheets, and slept comfortably until morning.

In the morning, the hand appeared again and a voice said, "Well done, young man! You are very brave. Until now, no one who has come to this place has dared to follow me. If you lie still in that bed for three nights, no matter what should happen, you may free a king's daughter from captivity and yourself become a king."

Abbas was willing to endure anything to free a king's daughter. That evening he feasted at the table again, then he went to bed. At the stroke of midnight, the doors of his room opened and in came several men with clubs, who beat him all over until he was black and blue. He felt as if every bone in his body was broken, and he was sore and afraid. But in the morning the hand appeared again, bringing magical medicines to heal his wounds and food to sustain him, and he was soon well.

On the second night he feasted at the table again, but after he had gone to bed the men came in at midnight and beat him more sorely than the night before. In the morning he could not lift his head from the pillow, but the hand appeared again and brought the medicines to soothe and heal him and food to sustain him, and he recovered.

On the third night things went the same way, and although he was close to death, he bore the punishment in silence. But the next morning he waited in vain for the hand to appear. And he began to give up all hope and prepared to die. Then, quietly, the door opened and in came a beautiful girl. She bathed his wounds with a magic lotion, which healed them at once. Then he got up and dressed and went to breakfast. The lovely girl sat down beside him. They ate together, but Abbas could not take his eyes off her, so great was her beauty.

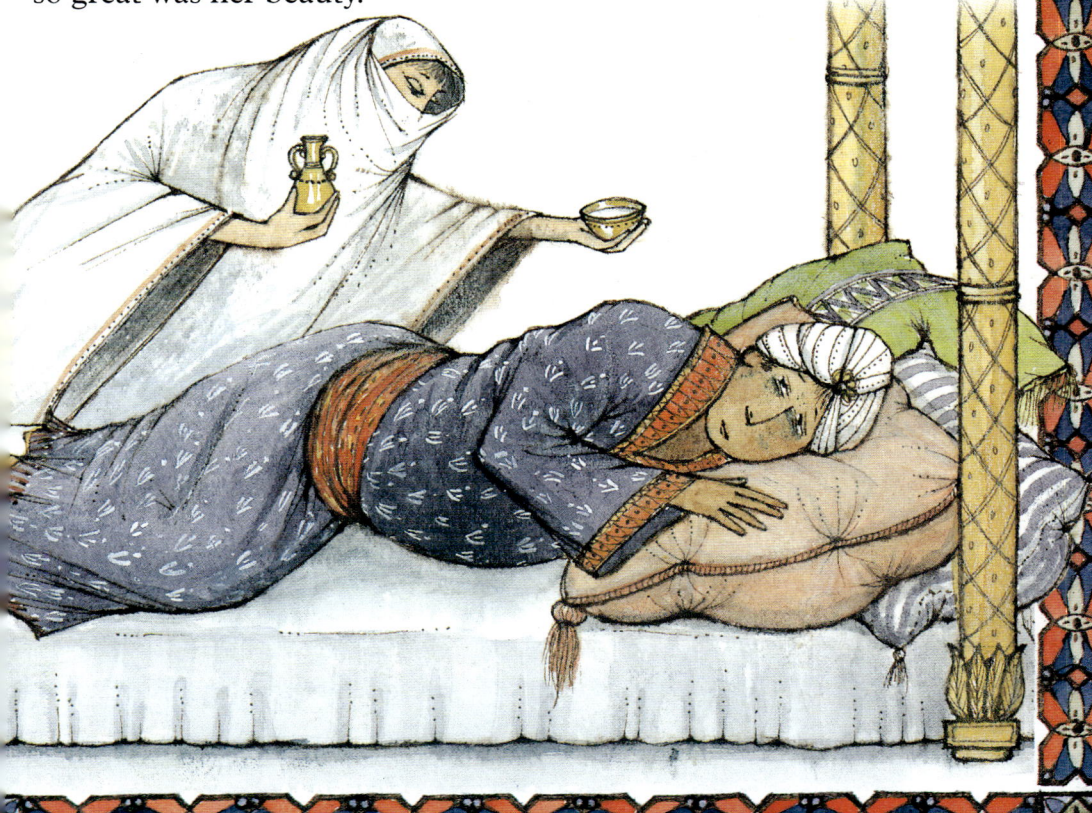

After a while he asked her who she was.

"I am the daughter of the King of Morocco," she said. "The Jinns made me a captive here, and until now no one was able to rescue me. Each man who has come to rescue me has run away after the first night of beatings. So I have been a prisoner here for years, and I have seen no one. I have been longing to see my father and mother. You are the first one to bear the beating with patience. The spell is broken now, and you must follow me to my father's palace."

No sooner had she said these words than the princess vanished from before his eyes, and Abbas found himself in his old clothes once more in the ruins of the castle. He was in great distress, but he made up his mind to seek her and follow her to her father's palace. Since he had no money in his pocket and no other way to get there, he had to walk—which, of course, took a very long time!

After the princess reached the palace, she waited and waited for Abbas, but he did not turn up, and she wondered if he had forgotten her. Day after day she kept her eyes on the road, but still Abbas did not come. At last, she gave up hope and grew tired of waiting. She agreed to marry a prince who had wanted her badly for a long time.

The day came for her wedding. The horses stood waiting, tossing their heads and pulling on their reins. Just as the princess put her foot on the step of the coach, she saw Abbas in his ragged clothing waiting at the palace gate, and she recognized him. He looked up at her sadly, for he could see that he had arrived too late to marry his beautiful princess. But the girl turned to the prince and said, "A little while ago I lost the key of my diamond chest. Afterwards I had a new one made, but then I found the old one. Now which of them should I use?"

And the prince said, "Clearly, you should use the old one."

Then the princess reached down, took Abbas by the hand, and said to the prince, "See! This is the one I meant when I spoke to you about the old key. He rescued me from the palace of the Jinns when I had no prince, and I promised to marry him. Please, my lord, go marry someone else."

The prince could find no words with which to answer the girl's demand. Her father, too, was astounded when he saw what a ragged and dirty young man his daughter had chosen in place of a prince.

The prince said to the girl, "It is for you to choose between us." Of course, she chose Abbas.

The King gave his consent, and they had a splendid wedding.

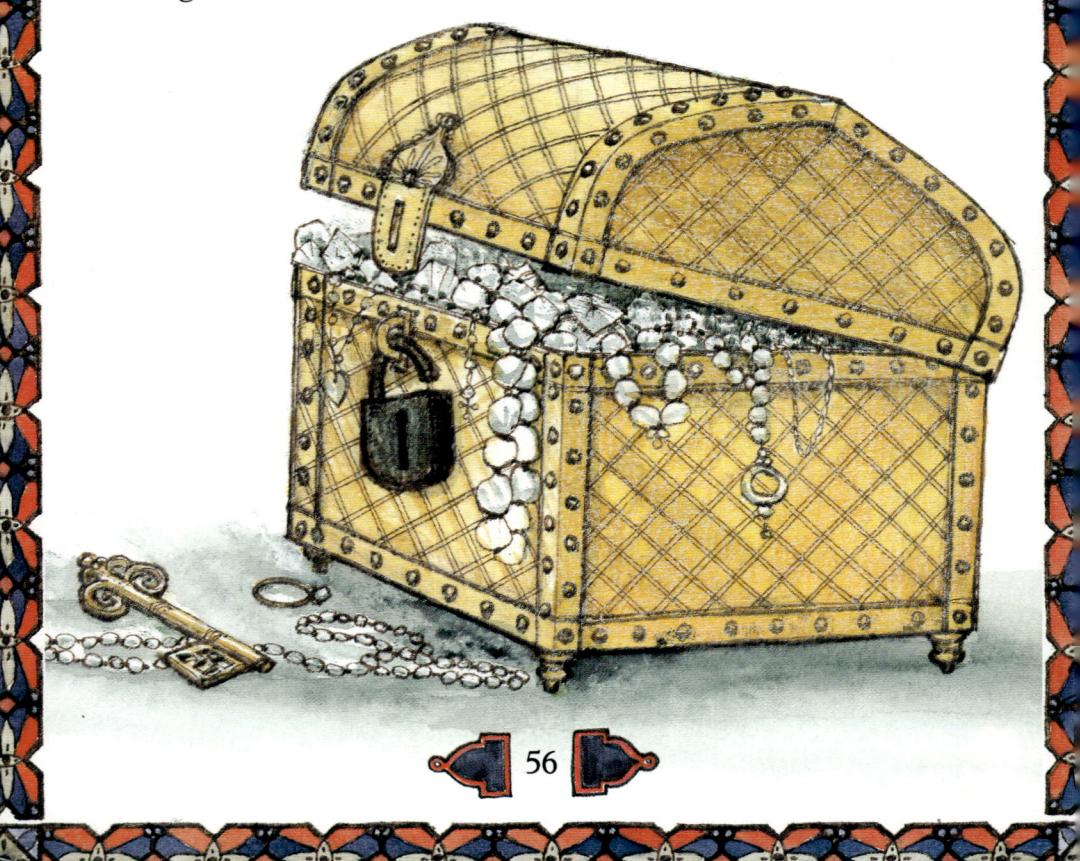